SWAVORY

Poems For Our

Daughters

Akira
my sister, my
friend, my mother...
I thank you for including
me in the musical that is your
life. Keep penning and one day soon you
will break through!
love you do life!
Trina Leshay

By:

Trina-Leshay Johnson

"Poetrina"

Swavory

<u>Dedications</u>

To:

Destiny Leshay Doxey
Happy 16th Birthday

To:

Vivian Charlene Williams
1970-1980

To:

Daughters of all ages
You Are My
Swavory Sisters

Swavory

Table Of Contents

In-Tro

Swavory

Swavory was born from a gift poem from a mother to her daughter. This poem was to be presented on the daughter's 16th birthday – the one most commonly known as the Sweet 16. But this mother was a little, well, different. This mother wanted to offer her daughter an opportunity to be more than sweet on this monumental day. So this mother presented her daughter with the gift of Swavory.

Swavory is what comes from being both sweet and savory.The poems in this book are for all daughters – both young and old. Daughters who are up for the challenge to:

Be both sweet **and** savory
Sweet and Savory
Swavory

Welcome to the Swavory Sisterhood

Swavory

Personal Dedication Page

To:

_____

From:

_____

Date:

_____

Swavory

Swavory

I give you permission
Not to be sweet
Unless of course
You want to be
      You really want to be

In that case
Be the sweetest possible
The sweetest sweetie
You can be

      But let me offer you an option
            An alternative to being sweet
                An opportunity not be sweet
                    To not be only sweet

Why not add a little savory
Yes some savory

Savory as in
Spicy
Savory as in
Aromatic
Savory as in
Zesty

      Full of flavor
      Full of punch
      Full of life
      Full of power

Swavory

Let me offer you
    An another option
        An alternative

Be both sweet **and** savory
    Sweet and Savory
        Swavory
            Swavory
                I give you permission

Be sweet **and** savory
    Be swavory
        Swavory
            Be whatever
            You choose

Be creative
    Be wild
        Be free
            Be you
                Be *swavory*

Swavory

Reflections

I was created to be...

_____

_____

_____

_____

_____

_____

_____

_____

_____

_____

_____

_____

_____

_____

_____

_____

_____

_____

_____

_____

_____

Swavory

Risk

Risk in the healing process is the place where the rubber meets the road. The foundations of trust and care have been laid and now comes the time to put the flesh on the bones and take a chance!

Risk is the door through which one must move in order for change to begin her healing work. I risk stepping into the worlds of those who are hurting and ask them to cast their words like spells – love potions for the self.

I ask for those who long to be healed to scatter their words like seeds that will one day become medicinal plants to be carried in their pouches along the remainder of life's journey.

I want to be healed
But the way is unclear
The bridge from
Bondage to freedom
Appears to be rickety at best

I want to be healed
But I can't see the way
The bridge from
Broken to whole
Is tattered and torn

The bridge is not solid
Nor is it made of stone
This bridge is as old as time
And looks to be
Worn thin
Almost invisible

Swavory

I want to be healed
But I don't know how
Don't know how
To make it
Across this dilapidated bridge

Cast your words like spells
In front of you
Scatter your words like seeds
Before each step
Weave you words like a tapestry
Across the bridge
To pave the way

Don't look down
Nor to the left or right
Keep your eyes focused
And your feet moving forward

Embrace the fear
And keep casting
Keep throwing
Keep creating
Keep weaving
The words that come
From your soul

Soul words
Will fill in the gaps
Soul words
Will guide your way
Soul words
Will get you to the other side

Swavory

I want to be healed
But the way is unclear
The outcome unknown

I want to be healed
So I cast
And I scatter
And I weave

     I want to be healed

Swavory

Reflections

I will take the risk to heal…

_____

_____

_____

_____

_____

_____

_____

_____

_____

_____

_____

_____

_____

_____

_____

_____

_____

_____

_____

_____

_____

_____

_____

_____

Swavory

First Steps

I heard the first step was a dozy
But damn!
I landed flat on my face.

Flat on my face
In the middle of the street.
Damn that hurt!

I want to just sit here
But then I'll just get run over,
So I get up

Wobbly
Shakily
Apprehensively
I get up and keep trying
Trying first steps

First steps towards
              Healing
                First steps towards
                          Wholeness
                                First steps towards
                                          Hope

Gingerly
Cautiously
Fearfully
It hurts but I keep trying
Trying first steps

Swavory

First steps towards
       Unknown places
           First steps towards
               Unbelievable possibilities
                    First steps towards
                        Unimaginable dreams

Curiously
Craftily
Boldly
Getting close but not there yet

Trying first steps

First steps towards
       Recovery
           First steps towards
               Re-invention
                    First steps towards
                        Redemption

Gracefully
Creatively
Bravely
I can't stop trying
Trying first steps

First steps towards
       Tangibility
           First steps towards
               Totality
                    First steps towards
                        Tremendous

Swavory

I heard the first step was a dozy
But damn that hurt!

I get up and keep trying
It hurts but I keep trying

Getting close but not there yet
I can't stop trying
Trying…

Trying first steps

Swavory

Reflections

I am taking first steps towards…
_____

_____

_____

_____

_____

_____

_____

_____

_____

_____

_____

_____

_____

_____

_____

_____

_____

_____

_____

_____

Swavory

Windows

All I want is a window
A window of my very own

All I want is a window

A window to look out into the world
A window to look deeply into the soul

All I want is a window

To stand in front of and dream
To curl up in front of and create
To sit in front of and write

All I want is a window

A window open wide to opportunities
One open wide to my hopes
Open wide to my dreams
A window open wide to the possibilities

All I want is a window

A window framed by peace
Fabricated by joy
A window bordered by freedom
Surrounded by grace
A window constructed by love

All I want is a window

Swavory

A window that will allow me to see many visions
A window that will allow me to hear many voices
A window that will allow me to taste many delicacies
A window that will allow me to feel many touches
A window that will allow me to smell many aromas

    All I want is a window

A window packed of promise
A window plump with prospects
A window percolating with power
A window pulsation with passion

    All I want is a window

A window through which I can leap
A window through which I can fly
A window through which I can soar

    All I want is a window
        To revision our future
           To imagine a new way of being

    All I want is a window
        One of my very own

        All I want is a window
          All I need is a window…

Swavory

Reflections

All I need is a window…

_____

_____

_____

_____

_____

_____

_____

_____

_____

_____

_____

_____

_____

_____

_____

_____

_____

_____

_____

Swavory

Become What You Believe

Once upon a time there was a you
A smaller you with big, clear dreams
A younger you with perfect vision for your future
A you that had a focused belief in anything being possible

But over time your sight gradually began to slip
Little by little
The clarity began to cloud
Little by little
The sharpness began to fade
Little by little

Your brain tried it's best to make everything appear as it should
Look like it was supposed to look

Your brain was working overtime
And so over time you began it believe that this trick was true
You got used to the blurry
Got used to the lack of detail
Used to the color lose

Then one day you realized
        Your vision was completely gone
            Gradually it had left you
                Your perfect vision was now lost

Blind – without your vision
Groping in the dark for direction
Pretending you could still see
Turning this way and that

Trying to catch the hope of recovery
From this voice

Swavory

Telling you to come this way
No, that voice
Telling you to go over there

But after awhile
You got tired of running into the walls
And tripping over the obstacles
So you decided to play it safe and just sit down

There you sat
In the darkness
With no vision
With no hope

When all of sudden you hear a voice coming towards you
Yes, you can still hear

On that day
It was this voice that gave you hope
On that day
You heard the words
"Become what you believe"

On that day
You regained your vision
Because on that day
You believed
So on that day
You became

That day can be this day
If you can once again perceive

This day can be the day
When you become what you believe

Swavory

Become what you believe
Whatever that may be

Become what you believe
Cast your vision for all to see

Become what you believe
The Master says it is so

Become what you believe
It will be better than you know

Once upon a time there was a you
A you with big, clear dreams

A you with perfect vision for your future

A you that had a focused belief in anything being possible

And you lived happily ever after
Because through it all
You became what you believed yourself to be

Swavory

Reflections

I believe… _____

_____

_____

_____

_____

_____

_____

_____

_____

_____

_____

_____

_____

_____

_____

_____

_____

_____

_____

_____

Swavory

Forget About It

You remember that woman in all the old scary movies
The one who always fell down
While running from the monster

Yeah you know the one
The one who when she started to run
We all knew she was about to die
You know, the one who was always looking back

She was too busy looking back
To make it out of her mess
Looking back like she forgot what
The thing that was after her looked like

Always too busy
Looking back
To get very far ahead

You remember her
I know you do
Especially because you probably saw her yesterday

Yesterday, in your very own reflection
Now how did that happen?
How did she become you ?

Well, you started looking back
Looking back while trying to run forward
Now you know that ain't gonna work

When, you ask, did you become that one?
When, you ask, did you put a limit on your time?
When did you trip over that thing on the ground?

Swavory

When did you fall down and find that you couldn't get up?

When you started looking back

But wait let me tell you how you can fix this mess
Let me tell you what you gotta do
Forget about it
Yeah that's the ticket
Forget about it
And you just might live
Forget about that man that promised to love you forever, ever
Forget about that woman that crushed the mess out of your heart
Forget about that job that was supposed to be your security

Forget about the shame
Forget about the pain
Forget about the fear
Forget about the betrayal
Forget about the negativity you allowed yourself to hear

Forget about the success
Forget about the failure
Forget about the right
Forget about the wrong
Forget about tears in the middle of the night

Forget about the left down
Forget about the get down
Forget about the set up
Forget about the mess up

And then forget that someone once told you that you could never
forget

Swavory

God forgets and so can you
God forgets and so can you
God forgets and so can you

But don't you dare
Forget about what I'm telling you
Cause holding on to all that stuff
Is only holding you back

Back from your present
Back from your future
Back form your right now
Back from your could be

And if for some reason you won't
For fear of what might happen
Remember home girl from the scary movies
Who when she started to run
We all knew she was about to die
You know, the one who was always looking back

You gotta forget so that you can see clearly what is ahead
See what it is you are reaching, stretching and straining towards
See that it can be achieved

Forget about it and press
Forget about it and press
Forget about it and press

Press towards your freedom!
Press towards your healing!
Press towards your forgiveness!
Press towards your love!
Press towards your life!

Forget about it!

Swavory

Reflections

I choose to forget about...

_____

_____

_____

_____

_____

_____

_____

_____

_____

_____

_____

_____

_____

_____

_____

_____

_____

_____

_____

_____

_____

Voice

I see your struggle
As you fight to survive

I hear your pain
As fear pours from your eyes

I feel your heart
As your blood flows cold with grief
    As your tears flood the bloodstained ground

As you cry
I cry too

As you cry
From a broken heart

As you cry
Over shattered dreams

As you cry
About an uncertain future
I cry too

I cry out
Because I want to help

I cry out
Because I want to heal

I cry out
Because I want to hold

Swavory

I cry out
Because you cry
      Because you cry
          Because you cry

I see your struggle
As you fight to survive

I hear your pain
As fear pours from your eyes

I feel your heart
As your blood flows cold with grief
      As your tears flood the bloodstained ground

As you cry
I cry too

As you cry
From a broken heart

As you cry
Over shattered dreams

As you cry
About an uncertain future
I cry too

I cry out
Because I want to help

I cry out
Because I want to heal

I cry out

Swavory

Because I want to hold
I cry out

    Because you cry

       I cry out

         Because you cry

          Because you cry

           I Cry Out!

Swavory

Reflections

I cry out for...
_____

_____

_____

_____

_____

_____

_____

_____

_____

_____

_____

_____

_____

_____

_____

_____

_____

_____

_____

_____

_____

Swavory

Pull It Together

Chips of bone
Specks of matter
Drops of blood

Sweep around
Sweep around the room for
Flecks of the profane
Fragments of the wild
Crumbs of the carnal
Scraps of the tribal

      Pull it together
      Pull it all together

Things that don't seem to go
Things that capture
Things that release
Things that muddy
Things that clear

Gather in one place
All that has been pulled together
And watch the fusion
Become the new norm
And become free
Become whole

      Pull it together
      Pull it all together

Swavory

Reflections

I need to pull together…

_____

_____

_____

_____

_____

_____

_____

_____

_____

_____

_____

_____

_____

_____

_____

_____

_____

_____

_____

Swavory

In The Valley

With You
I have run up and down the mountains
I have forced my way through the winds and the rains

With You
I have fought the giants
I have slain fears
I have overcome
I have been overcome
I have…with You

I come now to the valley
And before I walk through it
I will rest

Before I move on to the next quest
Face the next hurdle
I rest

Lay down my shield
Put away my sword
Rest

Rest in the valley's shadow
Lay down in its chill
Drink in its darkness
Hide amongst its undergrowth

Hide so that I might heal

Heal in its mud
Drench myself in its essence

Swavory

Be comforted by its closeness

Be soothed by its coolness

Be covered by its grit

Be healed
In the valley

Be healed
And rest

In the valley

Swavory

Reflections

I find rest..
_____

_____

_____

_____

_____

_____

_____

_____

_____

_____

_____

_____

_____

_____

_____

_____

_____

_____

_____

_____

_____

Swavory

Unbreakable

You've got everything you need
You just need to find it
It was with you,
"In the beginning"
You just need to be reminded
That it's yours

Your birthright
Your heritage
Your legacy

> You are unbreakable!

The outsides are
> Bendable
> > Stretchable
> > > Bodily harmable, oh yes

But the insides
Your insides
Thrives under pressure
Immensely unfathomable

Your insides
Rise in the face of heat
Excruciatingly unbelievable

Your outsides will grow weary
Your outsides will cry in pain
Your outside will waste away

Swavory

But your insides
Your insides will never faint
Never give in
Never die

                Never!

You've got everything you need
You need only remember
Your birthright
Your heritage
Your legacy

                You are unbreakable!

Your outside may appear as coal
But your inside is as a diamond

Untamable

      Unshatterable

          Unshakable

             Unbelievable

                Unbreakable

Swavory

Reflections

Inside of me…

_____

_____

_____

_____

_____

_____

_____

_____

_____

_____

_____

_____

_____

_____

_____

_____

_____

_____

_____

_____

_____

Out-Tro

Now is your turn

Your turn to speak

Speak your words

Step fully into the sisterhood

Add your presence

Add your voice

Add your Swavoryness

Swavory

Speak Your Words

_____

_____

_____

_____

_____

_____

_____

_____

_____

_____

_____

_____

_____

_____

_____

_____

_____

_____

_____

_____

_____

_____

Swavory

Swavory

Swavory

Swavory

Swavory

Swavory

Swavory

Swavory

Swavory

Swavory

Contact Me

Phone: (619) 566-6171

Email: PoeTrina@speakyourwords.net

Twitter: @poetrinaleshay

Facebook: www.facebook.com/speakyourword

Website: www.SpeakYourWords.net

Swavory